In Case You Get This

A Collection of Poems

by

Cheryl Hopson

Finishing Line Press
Georgetown, Kentucky

In Case You Get This

A Collection of Poems

Copyright © 2023 by Cheryl Hopson
ISBN 979-8-88838-284-4 First Edition
All rights reserved under International and Pan-American Copyright Conventions. No part of this book may be reproduced in any manner whatsoever without written permission from the publisher, except in the case of brief quotations embodied in critical articles and reviews.

ACKNOWLEDGMENTS

"Conversation Begets" was originally published in the *Toronto Quarterly*.
"A Sunday Afternoon of Listening to Lionel Richie Sing" was originally published in *The Indianapolis Review*.
"On Origins" and '#hertoo' were originally published in *Third Stone Journal*

Publisher: Leah Huete de Maines
Editor: Christen Kincaid
Cover Art and Design: Kentucky artist Kasey Curtis-Petrocelli
Author Photo: Cheryl Hopson

Order online: www.finishinglinepress.com
                also available on amazon.com

Author inquiries and mail orders:
Finishing Line Press
P. O. Box 1626
Georgetown, Kentucky 40324
U. S. A.

Table of Contents

Adolescence, 1980s 1
And Last Week I Told Myself 3
I Have Been Afraid 4
Something to Be Reckoned With 5
The Night Before 6
Worry Seems 7
I Stand Before These Beautiful Things 8
I Keep Coming Back 9
By Your Words 10
You Can't Drink It Away 11
I Feel My Lion 12
Forever Means Forever 14
Conversation Begets 15
Untitled #1 16
Untitled #2 17
Family Acrostic 18
Caramel Cakes, Rainstorm, and Casualties 19
Show Yourself, Father, and Account For This 20
I Stopped Asking Why 21
Am I Depressed? 23
1985 (A Poem in Memory of Viola) 24
Not Symbiosis, But— 25
Spring 2001 26
If I Could Tell You Anything 27
Untitled #3 28
Where Did You Go? 29
We Are Not Strangers 30
Untitled #4 31

Untitled #5 32
A Sunday Afternoon of Listening to Lionel Richie Sing 33
On Origins 34
#hertoo 35
In Case You Get This 36
Untitled #6 37
On Grief 38
Untitled #7 39
Tonight's the Night 40
Mourning, Still 41
And, Still, I Go On Missing You 42
Day One 43
Once Upon a Time 44
What Is Love? 45
What It Means to Lose You 46
Listen, ... 47
A Variation on Theme 48
My First Therapist 49
Singing Aretha 50
On Losing II 51

To Tameca
("forever, for always, for love" —L.V.)

Adolescence, 1980s

I'm on edge, still
Every year leading up to now
Every conversation had or avoided
Every forced and feigned interaction. Step
Family in the age of Reaganomics
in the era of crack cocaine and
women with children becoming perfect
(victimized) facades
to hide behind or hang on
"Respectable" and all the while
the insides turned, rotting, and
You broke it. No.
You found it broken
and saw a future who knows
a roof over your head a woman to bully
food in your belly who knows
who knows and by now the care irks
and who am I to judge, except
the Trauma formed from that
particular kind of
heterosexual love
dynamic, and
being a child in-development
then, developing
in the midst of
adults still feeling unloved
and hating on their mothers, still
experiencing Rejection, and
hating on their father's
father's father's father, and
I am The same eyes
of that six year old
girl seen too much

and I alone
made it

out alive, and
nothing but the memory remains,
still.

And Last Week I Told Myself

and last week I told myself
The treacheries of the past,
not a past in which I was innocent, except
what should one Expect
of a five, eight, and twelve-
Year-old in the face of
a crack epidemic lived out
in her home? A decade-delayed
diagnosis of a perilous Patriarchal
others' disorder
become the Order of
our living?

What is anger in the face of
The end to an "(over)long Prison
sentence" of a child-
hood?

Do I hate?
Does hatred fill me?

Does hatred fill me?

I Have Been Afraid

I have been afraid of her.
I have feared her emotions,
her premature death.

I have feared being made responsible for her,
have feared having to replace her.
I have feared her burdens.

her despotism
and insights on
daughters, and
in particular
me—

I feared her.

I loved her
With a heaviness of heart, a
Divided self and
Mind, and, in time,
An oceanic rage that broke
And breaks levees
Meant to shore up and contain what is natural,
what will come, what cannot be
forgotten,
forgiven,
or
denied,

again.

Something to Be Reckoned With

Most days, these days

it is impossible to focus

I think of the late Toni Morrison and
Remember what she writes about racism
Being a distraction.

I need to get back
To travails with Zora and to music
Zora's sister, Sarah, might have
done the good get down to
and the car that Zora drove,
and the people
Like West and Cullen and Hughes
Zora crossed and
intersected with and
film and folklore Zora made,
stuff,
and Kamala Harris won
and Stacey Abrams is a national
treasure, and the mayor of Atlanta
Is a Black woman named Kesha. And
I see now that what people (yeah,
you Know) hate is our style,
our Intelligence,
our creativity,
and hope, our
Joy- and this also,
our Organizing, and
Our power—

Which says
We Are

Something to Be
Reckoned With.

The night before

We watched Indiana
Jones from 1989 and
River Phoenix came back
To mind again, and
We sent a verbal salute,
And rest easy to Sean
Connery and I left the
Scene early to go work
At the braces on my teeth,
For three more months
Promises my orthodontist and
Thank everything as I'm
Ready to be done and
Now we're watching Martin
Crane complain about his
Love life while the world outside
Burns and churns on and yes,
I'm agitated, and
Yes, I require several
Breaks from being anything
To anyone full time nonstop and
Otherwise cannot stand
Or sit and listen to or tolerate
Much. Much. And this is
Much. These rebel whites are
Not harmless they are not fun or funny
They are not—

Worry Seems

Worry seems
an unnecessary Burden
too heavy to hold, and
otherwise unneeded.

I've been taking day breaks
after Years of nonstop
laboring For this foothold
this post Moment
following a life First, a
family first,
a First, and there will never
be another For this, this
laying it all out This celebration
and this Recognition of My
Tenured
and
Promotable
Work.

Lord, these nerves
Though.

"I stand before these beautiful things [1]

"pictures of my family, framed and scattered"
"The sharp blue light of this cold winter day"
"MILK, the movie"

"You learn more from
what makes you laugh" and
"How much pleasure the tongue
can bring"

"Life Lessons."

"It is not as if
the struggle is useless, it's that
it continues"

"good job"
"On past accounts / overdue"

"Negro citizens"
and

"murderous smug whites"

"It's as if
all gifts come all at once / like
the way the sun breaks
through dark
clouds. / You just look up, smiling"

---

[1] All lines for the poem are taken from Patricia Spears Jones's *A Lucent Fire* (2015).

I Keep Coming Back

I keep coming back to
The look on your face the first time,
The "I will not explain myself
To you" look that made and makes me want
To put a gate around my heart
So that there is no grief when I strike back
No guilt or wondering, a gate to keep your
Watering eyes (too late!) from moving me
Beyond this generational and particular race and
Gender and sexuality and class and caste
Rage, the kind that wants to take your developed
Head into both my hands and shake it
Until the stupid loosens, until the rightness
That is your own idea of whiteness reflects back to
You the damage done. But you are protected
From my wrath, are swaddled in accolades and
Championed as a visionary and all I can say at this stage
Is what goes around comes around

By Your Words

By your words your
Inaction, your
Animosity, solipsism,
And even
Screams

And
At your age.

I'm
Looking out, beyond this
Feeling of being disliked
In love. Beyond
The limitations of
This choice, and
choosing.

You can't drink it away.

Eat it away.
Sex it away.
Laugh it away.
Hope it away.
Lie it away.
Ignore it away.
Travel, sleep, or work it away.
It's yours now.
It's yours.
I know you don't want it.
I know you resent that's it's
Real. I know and there
Is nothing else to say
Except you are as well as can be,
considering—and grateful
To be left with a charge—"Write
Our story," and
A blessing, "I love you just the way
You are" but fuck that, just
Live.

I feel my lion

Self, listening to "My
Power," and can see with
My sovereign eye

the sovereign
Self, stripped
Naked and plentiful
With stories
Of trauma and
Treasure.

"They feel a way.
Oh, wow."

This is just to say,
I'm coming
To collect every dollar stolen
from me.

Your reign,
a blinding white
Suffocating light
Shielding the filth
and crimes of men
(and their women, ad infinitum)
deemed "fathers"
and "Founders".
Of what?

Anyway,
The debt is due and
if I were you,
I'd figure out
Quick
how to
settle up.

In the meantime: I am
not a machine. I
have never been dumb. You
are not the first
attempted murderer of me and
more to the point
of the woman you fant-
asize/d , and with such limited
imagination

how you prove yourself dumb
and not "Good," or "Great,"
the way the acolytes
Proclaim, but
average, or worse—

Would-be killer,
I feel my strength again
After the looting of me and
Mine, and I know now
the ways Your harm has transformed
Me but not before the Weakening,
and the Shock—to be debased in the name
of Groupthink, and idolatry. As Mariah sings, "I ain't
the type to play the martyr" and
at this age. And,
at this age.

Forever Means Forever—

Morning, just at or around
9, cloudless; a perfect canvas for what might
Have been a perfect day. Babies on field trips, and other Beloveds, and crumbling buildings, fire
Balls, leaping people, and
dust. Those
In the vicinity said they could smell burning flesh,
And the Black woman covered in dust died years later at 42.
This remembering
Must be
passed on,
collected
in books, where words open up to hold it,
To pass along
what losing
And pain
and love look like
Up close,
so close our days become
Forever changed, and

Forever means forever—

Conversation Begets

Sister,

Poets get born and baptized by word and
blessings follow.

Yesterday you talked
of Sartre and Camus and 'American' existentialism, voicing air quotes, and
I, six hours away nodded, keeping time.

And there were times
when I thought: some things reconfigure and change; some things remain
the same.

I thought about Sartre, Camus, and You, U.S. Black and
educated woman in crisis—

And this is what I wanted to say: Sister, when we talk
let us speak on things to help each other remember. Let's not speak of
Sartre and Camus.

Sister, there is an image of a black woman that repeats for me. She is the
wife of a man killed
in the September 11 "bombings" and
she is holding a picture of her husband and
she is saying: "This man was my life. I lived for him,"
and her voice is breaking, and snippets of her grief
are showing and the sound is manifesting the pain and I am let inside and
there is heat, and her hurt
is unyielding.

Sister, when we talk,
let's help each other remember
our worth.

Untitled #1

I want so much
Back, like laughter between us,
Like a safe space to fall, like
nobody sick in the body
in the head
in the heart and so
the laughter is real
so real
people stop to listen, to listen
and to become again
a human being who does human things
and somehow has hope.

Untitled #2

I tried to put words on it
so I could study it
so that whatever it was
would move through my body,
killing off its deadened parts
but I sat in silence
in tears, muttering, trying to
cull letters into sound, and
I did not raise my voice
so much as tremble, wondering at
our different days
and wanting to be happy,
and knowing the impossibility
of living as free, and
mourning, still.

Family Acrostic

Let's lock hands and
Out ourselves to a world
Vying for space in our
Everyday. Let's
Rise in this love.

Caramel Cake, Rainstorm, and Casualties

What I took to be a Jamaican-American woman with a machete
turned out to be a rainbow on asphalt
showing off after a summer rainstorm;
and what I took to be a four-layered caramel cake
wrapped in wax paper and crumbling
turned out to be my Grandmother Vivian's
aged hands removing the cellophane from a peppermint.
It was my brain fooling me,
sending me false images,
turning rotting green apples and
levees into marigolds,
"and it was my brain that betrayed me completely,
sending me entirely encoded material,"
for what I thought was a book of poetry
turned out to be the last card my sister would ever send me, with a note in her hand,
and what I thought was a stinkbug on the front door screen
turned out to be a chickadee midflight
and what I thought was, at last, The Wisdom of the Centuries
turned out to be 140,000 casualties and
still no cure.

Show Yourself, Father, and Account for This

I.   How could you let it happen let the life slip out of them and without me there to catch and pour it back in? How could you take my loves away from me? And nothing in the world can fix it. Nothing in This world, no magic to reverse the curse of death, and dying. And I blame you tonight and for the sake of sleep. I do everything but call you out of your name, and I am burning with fire. You let them go. You let them leave Me, LEAVE us, and we are in shambles.

II.   You ever yelled at god in a poem
kicked and screamed and thrown all kinds of
fit. Picked up the nearest word and smashed it
against the wall by Her head, by where you imagine His
head to be? all while talking about
HOW COULD YOU and LET THEM
LEAVE? And WITHOUT ME there to raise a voice or
lift a hand to say, NO. STOP. STAY
without me there to wash their faces clean,
to open up their eyes again and bring them back
to me? You ever said, SHOW YOURSELF,
Father, and account for this?

I Stopped Asking Why

For the life of me
I had to get beyond
needing to know
The reason/s

Reason is a trick of the mind
and bends and tells nothing much
like what time of day it was
or what you were wearing and
How you felt in your skin and
Whether you were with a coworker
Or friend when
it came to you
that
Your life is yours
and that what happened was unfair
And left you near-crazed and ready to surrender

Nerves frayed, tired,
Afraid, you built
a shrine,
pride be damned

And I watched you,
Young and heady
Burdened with trauma and
The left behind, and
I learned that women perform
for the men in their lives
Men who carry them
in their pockets,
And keep a vice grip on
Their minds
And
even though the red flag was up,
signaling that the water was unsafe,
I saw you relinquish

Yourself to cresting waves,
And you, unable to swim

Am I Depressed?

There are less than ten days until March.
I am almost four years from fifty.
I continue to untangle from my mother.
I continue to write and revise myself.
I talk to myself in the shower. Like
Doppelgänger to Self, like Id, Ego,
Superego and Shadow, there is a back and
Forth exchange by which I come to clarity
Or delusion, who's to say? I am grieving
I can feel the empty space of them,
Of all of us alive and then the gush of wind
The cold let in and into my bones. They are gone
Forever gone, and one day I will be too. Sorrow
Ain't sweet, and I'll tell you something else it's downright annoying,
Stepping on your toe in high heels, blowing secondhand
Smoke in your face. Sorrow is rotgut and a thief and I hate it,
A strong word to match a feeling I want to stomp out, but
I'm no fool, and them so far
Gone, gone, and nothing to bring them back no
Sorcery or pagan worship, no god of high or low,
no prayer nor magic spell, and words, yes, words
are something, and words no Words can never be enough
and I guess the answer is yes, I am depressed, and
damn mad about it.

1985 (A Poem In Memory of Viola)

The past is my treasure trove or my
Obsession. Every book read every modern-day
Prophet or guru teaches to leave it as you
Found it, under the murky blue green waters
Of the Gulf Coast or Atlantic, let the past remain
Sunken submerged beneath one refusal after another
And so on. Take a walk instead, skip, and
Keep your eyes focused on the step before you,
There will
Be resistances.

A familiar birdsong and the insinuating
Scent of honeysuckle and wet earth, a house
at the top of a winding gravel
Driveway in the countryside,
a screen door slammed without
Malice or intention, a voice raised then lowered,
a small yellow steel Formica table,
A red and white deck of cards,
become

my great aunt at home
at 65. Become a poem I
Continue all these years later
To build and construct, to
Write.

Not Symbiosis, But—

All my life has been a longing to
Connect with another and now I see that
It's not symbiosis I'm craving but oneness
The way two touch lives and become one and
For however short or long I don't want to own
You, or hold on too tight, and whatever rules
There are I want us alone to make and remake
There is no denying the way one body ____bends____\
Toward another, or mind wanders, skips, races down
Narrow streets and alley ways to get to to get to get
You, looking, listening, your eyes on mine
And us jiving like women who love
each other, two of a few thousand
doctor of philosophies writing
our life together "Bird by bird," and
so close to the dream some days it seems
foolish not to take note of a post-
4th noonday drive along I65, everything
Fecund green and freshly mowed
brown and black horses and rolling
Hillsides and the sun warm against
The window pane.

Spring 2001

A street fair   cotton candy   a
Windmill   narrow winding roads in a town in the South of France
hope in the in-between spaces of now and
becoming   Gray stone, blue skies, happy
impressions of faces against a backdrop of a
miniature Ferris Will.

It was bright out,
the middle of the day in May
and we (the three of us) were in love,
and with no idea
of what was coming.

If I Could Tell You Anything

May, not-yet-summer news of your death came
after some of the best news of my life.

And for weeks I could not cry,
and no words came out of my pen.

I sat in silence,
my head a prison
of thoughts of how
no one knows the particulars
of how you died, of how
at 34 I had written myself away
from where you lay,
away, and running.

Untitled #3

Looking back, I can see
The way youth shields the eyes and thus
The mind. The way clarity comes in waves
Cresting and still safe enough, we think,
Or at least hope, unless someone pushes open
A door with a scent used-to-be worn long time ago
By another and so scraping the bottom of your
Nose until your eyes begin to water, disappear
Into wetness and then close up shop—you
Hope because now the memory is here which
Means the person you try and tried hard to
Lance from your life and psyche with the sharpest
Blade, and no anesthetic or real training in
Doing so is wanting attention, and more—

Where did you go?

Where are you now?
What time did you leave, or does that matter?
Why am I crying?
What made me think of you?
Are you there?
Can you read this?
Yes, I am sad and that's part of it.
Yes, I am relieved you are no longer hurting.
No, I am not ok?
No, I am not fine.
I am sad, and missing you.
I am open to this sadness.
I know it will pass and come and pass until the end.
I am the oldest now going on 14 years
You know the story
There is no end to the shock.
I miss you, Sister.
Do you miss me?
I hope not.
I hope the book is closed on us, and this
On everything everything except
the children.

I miss you, sister. I wore dark matte
Lipstick today, knowing
You approved, and in genuflection to
The Tamecas of yore, and
The Tamecas to come.

Until the end,
Love.

We Are Not Strangers

We fight during the daylight
hours and just after nightfall I look at you
in silence trying to see around the invisible corners
of your clipped words, trying to read
the telegrammed message of your tears.

I shake off statistical data, push through
as this is all so foreign, except we are not
strangers to each other.

Untitled #4

This anger is Army of the Lord Righteous, is the senior choir marching in
On Sunday, is the bleach white of the usher Board uniforms, is the sweat
From Reverend Lee as he
Speak sings his way into and through another series of Y'all don't hear mes,
And Can I Get an Amens
I know this anger like I knew the routine of every Sunday
of my childhood with my Holiness grandmother.
I know the way this anger walks and Carries itself, and
I've seen it's scribbled private notes of
Anywhere but here. It's
a new old rage, and it wants to
Wreak havoc
to destroy good dishes and flat screen televisions,
to use up every drop of available hot water and leave you
Cold, and with nothing to warm you.

Untitled #5

Because of You,
I quit keeping silent to maintain peace

Question everything I do not see or hear on my own
Use up reservoirs of patience until bone dry
Insist on everything I know to be true
Trust in love, not foolishness.

A Sunday Afternoon of Listening to Lionel Richie Sing

This music, and the pungent sweet of honeysuckle
overrun in my love's backyard takes me back to
Sunday afternoons with my grandma; back to Holiness
Tabernacle Church of God in Christ; back to the
porch on Moorman Rd; back to my sisters
and my Grandma Vivian's hums—back
to that long-ago childhood in Virginia.

At 37 I returned on a Sunday in October
to bid farewell to the woman who introduced me
to God, and the same preacher of my youth studied
my black slacks and frowned.
Sundays during my childhood were never easy,
those hours of being held captive by Reverend's repeat commandment to
give until it hurts;
the constant question of grown folks—"Have you seen
your father?" asked with a perceivable glee.

I like the Sundays of my adult-life better—Lionel singing about
a need to be free.
No sermons of me perishing in flames for being me
no grandma willing her mind shut to empty already
Shallow pockets.

On Origins

Last night I dreamed that I, not my house but I was a stop
on the Underground Railroad, and I huddled masses in the bend and tuck
of my skirt and bellowed "Shhhh," and the safe space of I held, until
I sent them flying, fleeing not knowing
but trusting in the strength of the well-oiled collective, and I awoke, startled
by what was, for all intents and purposes, a nightmare—

Reverse me, She born 110 years before
the Emancipation Proclamation, born unfree to a woman born
unfree to a woman born free
and speaking an old tongue, carrying life that begot life, that begot
me, and I reverse the curse, end it.

#hertoo

I am coming for you
grown, and unafraid, I will
make you fear me, will
take a two-by-four of words
across your back, will bring you down
to your shot knees. My intention
is to do you harm
for the ways you broke
girls, trapped in a fantasy lived
out on their bodies.

Get ready.

In case you get this,

I am writing from my bedroom
On the night my sister called with news
Of you unresponsive, for a time, and
In ICU, and
How I would like to swallow up
All the time lost
Put a stopper on this countdown
We've been on without knowing

I want to talk to you
To touch you
To reach out to you and
Pull you back to this side— where I know
You're a phone call's distance, and
A plan ride away, and this pandemic
will pass and we will be standing
facing each other, again.

Untitled #6

I pushed the thought of you being gone
Away until I almost, almost
Forgot, until I could wake up in the morning
After and hearing birdsong, not rush to close out
The sound, until I could lift the blinds and receive
The blessing, baptismal sunshine, and step.
I cannot believe that you are gone.
Away from me,
Out of my hands,
Beyond my smile that made you smile,
Beyond me.

On Grief

Grief is many things including blindness,
grief buries the story of what happened
And to whom and when and oh, the horror
Somewhere deep within brain cells and blood cells
It saturates the body's organs and brands the mind
Such that nothing of the feeling of what was lost
Leaves, hides from view, cowers in the face of
New life and new possibilities, and
What else can we expect. Grief is Love is grief is love we're
Talking about and love and grief and grief and love
Belong I've learned to the human condition.

Untitled #7

I took the Myers-Briggs again
After twenty-five years.

By 38
I was fallow in a way that
Did not suggest life beneath the surface
Though life was there and building
Up and shoring up and because I come
From people who knew the land and they
Came from people who knew the land and
Lands I did not lose faith. Life is in me
And life has been in me for some time now
And so I took the famous personality test
Again after growing up and becoming
The thing dreamed of, the one at the center
Of a fantasy imaged by me, and made
Real. And the test reveals
I have CHANGED, or is it that
I've remained the same—

Tonight's the Night

Tonight's the night sang
Betty Wright and the people
Understood. Rehearsal is over. The
Show opens. Right here. On
This stage. Featuring you. An all-Black
Cast, and centering something more than
Words, the sauce of the song
with Betty on vocals and
The bass guitar starting out the
Tour of men on
Instruments making
Music, and Betty's voice making
Everything clear. It's time to Stan.
To put everything you've got and
Can get into on the table, and
Leave it there. Lay down some deep
And copious roots in already rich
And fertile soil. To go silent and
Be about action, to
Become something else
Altogether, and
once again.

And, Mourning, Still

I tried to put words on it so that
I could study and feel it and so that
Whatever it was would move through my
Body, killing off its deadened parts and
Reviving what remains but I sat in tears
And silence
muttering trying to
cull letters
Into sound, and I did not
Raise my voice so much as tremble
wondering
At our different days and wanting
to be happy and
knowing
the impossibility of living
Even now as free

And mourning still—

And, Still, I Go On Missing You

What is it about this moment that tells me
with certainty that what we are to one another,
because love is a continuous thing,
can never be lost; that everything is always
going to be alright; that love
persists, and
And
And

Still I go on missing you. Everyday. Feel
The missing in the center of my chest, know it
By the sense that I can't quite get right. So,
I dream. Fill in the space of your absence with
Cascading white waterfalls, green mountainscapes
And winding roads. You become the sound
of the ocean breaking at my feet, a bright yellow
Sweet lemon growing on a tree; you are
A piece of me, intertwined from the very start.

I dream of you, smiling. The noise about you
From troubled years gone quiet. A cool, soft blue
Hugs you, holds you until I can again.

Day One

And I deactivated my
Facebook account and feel
Unburdened by my Id by my
Ego by my Superego at battle
With one another, tedious tired
Constant right or wrong yes
Or no or who the fuck cares? Every
Body got a stake in the game a dog in
The race her finger on the red button
That ends and thus begins it all. I
Deactivated a shadow of a shadow of
Me that was always running his mouth and
carrying on like he don't care when this is
one of those gigs where whatever you called god
Ordained or through her made manifest and she mad
And tripping and 'bout to cause Creation to throw everything off
The bed, fitted sheets flats, duvets, pillows and all and dare you
To try and remake it in its old image which you forgot or never
Took the time to remember. I cut the cord the
Reverse umbilical where nutrients flowed out of me and
Ire and ego and mania flowed in. It's a start.

Once Upon A Time

I believed the performance in part because
Of your voice, a singers voice, the kind that invites
You inside the kind that bends your world alters
Reality makes you feel something bigger than yourself
In your own body I don't know how to say it,
I mourn, I wish for a different story, I try not
To turn away from the manipulation of the
Placating hand, the misery of separation remedied the best
Way possible in the moment, the touch says I see
You, says you're the one who matters, says the rest
Is necessary and distraction. You fooled me,
I'm not going to lie. I saw it with my own eyes but
Monkeys and carousels and Oprah interrupting you
And the music and Quincy. I must be missing
some version of you we together constructed, but
Maybe it is also that I miss myself in the past with you, a
Decade into the decline and with me young, and unknowing.
I guess what I'm saying is I miss the innocence of you
Who was for the five year old me cradling OFF THE WALL
Michael of the pretty brown skin ilk, Michael of the
Voice that called a little plump brown girl out into the world,
Michael of the smiling eyes, the one
Who knew and did no harm.

What Is Love?

Memory the faulty link the one storyline
We draw upon to structure and make sense of life
Which is to say of Creation, and no amount of moving
Around people like pieces on a game board and
No amount of wanting make any difference at all,
At all, at all. And
We love what we love and no amount
Of reasoning changes anything more than
Geography and choice which means the feeling remains
Which means love enacted is a rare thing
We hold firm to ideas of who we are built and
Handed on and adopted out of necessity or habit
Or worse, and or we wriggle free of the skin
We're in to become ourselves over and over
and over again. What is Love?
Too big a question for
One poem, or small enough to take some
Measure? Love is imperfect and an experience.
Love is seeing beyond our own yearning, it is
Trusting in the power of connection and
Reconnection, until the end,
To start.

What It Means to Lose You

I tried to write a poem about what it means to lose
you but the words never opened.
There was no light no bud,
nothing to nurse the seed or water
the soil. So I gave up, and now there's this
these words I commit to you each night
before dreams of our girlhood collapse
into a storyline that starts in the middle
and never ends. I remember colors
the wildcat blue of birds
the surprise of purple in a yard overgrown
with greenery; the dull brown
of fading winter cut through with
the yellow of the coming spring.

Listen,

because you may not know
or feel a thing, at first, and
so go on living like
nothing new has happened
under your sun, though
a bull has entered your
china shop, i.e., life,
and those who know
about bulls, and this one in particular
will feign innocence
and don indifference
when the bull let loose
does what bulls let loose
in china shops do, which is
tear up all of your shit,
chase you down and
lock its horns in you—chest, or ass
or knee; the bull is doing
what bulls do, when
the gate has been lifted, and
the bullfighter
and the clown
prove impotent,
and do nothing, or
Run.

A Variation on Theme

I speak
and tell a story
of losing
I am
a bridge
between, a variation
on theme, Lady Lazarus
with a made-up
face in varying shades
of black.

Where I'm from
is time
alone with my sisters,
grief, and
extravagant
demand.

My First Therapist

(*For* S.S.)

Singing along to Regina Belle singing Billie Holiday,
I am reminded of my first
Therapist, a Black woman I think I love—

My love for her is spiritual
is transference
and projection, is
also right on for real—
I mean, you know the kind of woman with
a PhD and a family legacy of
brick-by-brick
making it and investing in
herself and
brick-and-mortar

I watched her helping me to let go
to get some of my god
damn sass back,
to be that woman—

I fix/ed my hair better
I dress/ed better, and
love/d wiser. You hear that?
I said I love/d wiser.
She helped me with that
and let me cuss,
and cry, and
laugh—

This poem is
an official shout out.
She knows who
she is.

Singing Aretha

(A Poem in Memory)

Aretha wore gold and
was surrounded by pink-
ish white lavender
and a hint of purple
elegant and
perfect roses, perhaps
three hundred
or more, and that seemed right.
Her friends,
acquaintances,
colleagues,
and celebrity
others watched
and waited
as Aretha's family
came in, studied
the person in the casket,
sometimes blew her a kiss,
and moved on.
I sat at home watching
in the bright light
of our living room,
and the choir continued
to sing, and my eye caught sight
of a woman with a tambourine,
and I knew Aretha was taking us back
to her youth,
back to church, and
I remembered
my own child
self, unknowing
and singing
about "Chain
of Fools," singing

Aretha, circa 1983.

On Losing II

I notice the sadness and disinterest
And do not resist it, do not engage it,
Do not become it, I notice and focus in
And listen to what a part of me is wanting me to
Know, which is that losing without notice
And in successions quick is not felt in full
At first. No, it comes in days, and weeks—
Decades, and years.

Today I cobbled together dinner
For the two of us, and was satisfied
With myself for not spending when
There is food in the refrigerator and
An idea of what to cook and how

Today I wrote an abstract for a chapter
In an edited collection and the abstract
Was praised by the editor, which means,
In the spirit of the self-help gurus, I
GET to write a chapter on pedagogy and
Myself engaged in it

I don't know until I do that
I'm unsatisfied and missing you,
And have become a hostage
To what could have been,
and what was before the addiction
And dissembling, when direct eyes
Looked out on eyes, direct
and looking back.

Dr. Cheryl R. Hopson is an associate professor of English and African American Studies in the Department of English at Western Kentucky University in Bowling Green. Finishing Line Press published her chapbooks *Fragile* (2017) and *Black Notes* (2013). A scholar as well as a poet, she is currently writing a monograph of 20th century novelist and anthropologist Zora Neale Hurston. Her poems can be found in the *Toronto Quarterly*, the *Indianapolis Review, Not Very Quiet, Rise Up Review*; and more recently in the journal *Sinister Wisdom*.

www.ingramcontent.com/pod-product-compliance
Lightning Source LLC
Chambersburg PA
CBHW020934180426
43192CB00036B/1140